Speeches for Teenage Girls

Wilmington

Speeches for Teenage Girls

Susan Pomerance

Dramaline Publications

Copyright © 2005, Dramaline Publications.

All Rights Reserved.

Printed in the United States of America.

Dramaline Publications
36-851 Palm View Road
Rancho Mirage, CA 92270

Library of Congress Control Number: 2005925764

Cover art by Ann Dooley

This book is printed on paper that meets the requirements of the American Standard of Permanence of paper for printed library material.

CONTENTS

LISA

Lisa discovers what is real about someone and what is just appearance.

LISA

Yeah, well, I used to have these set ideas about people, you know. Used to judge them by the way they look and talk. Like this girl from India who was in my English class. Even though she was smart, she wore really dorky clothes and a bunch of weird-looking jewelry. And she spoke with this kinda sing-songy voice that made me feel embarrassed for her. Most of the kids ignored her and never spoke to her. Me included. I mean, who wants to be seen with some far-out foreign person, right?

Then one day, when I was trying to diagram a sentence, I made a real fool of myself in front of the class—I'm pretty lame when it comes to English. Anyway, I really goofed up and all the kids in the class were cracking up, which made me feel, you know, mentally challenged. Everybody except Indira. She didn't laugh or anything.

As I was leaving the room, Indira came up to me and told me she was really sorry for me and thought that people laughing at someone for not being good at something was rude and inexcusable. Then she said, if I wanted, she'd be glad to help me out. Like I said, she was super smart and a real whiz at English. So I told her okay and invited her over to my house after school.

Indira's been helping me out with my English for over a month now and I've really improved. She's a great teacher. And I found out that she's really a special person. But the thing I've learned way more than English or anything else is that it's really stupid to judge people before you get to know them.

ANGELA

Angela finds it difficult to find a boy to whom she can relate.

ANGELA

I don't know about you, Ellen, but too many guys are screw-ups. (*Pause.*) Yeah, not all, maybe, but way too many. It seems like it's getting harder all the time to find a guy who isn't a total jerk. Seems like we've become a jerk society. I don't know how my mom and dad ever hooked up.

When I asked her how she met Dad, she said it was at this roller rink. Roller rink! Is this ever corny or what? But corny or not, this is where they met and fell in love. And they hung together all through high school and college and after college got married. To me this is incredible. Maybe they were just lucky, I don't know. But I think things were a lot cooler back then. Mom said that what attracted her to Dad was that he was so mannerly and considerate. Wow! Most guys I meet are way too much into themselves, self-absorbed. Like Lanny Cartwright. We went together for a while, but when I was with him I felt like I wasn't important. All he ever talked about was himself and being good at basketball and how cool his clothes were. And when other girls were around I became invisible.

I don't know, maybe it's just me. Maybe my head's on crooked or I'm expecting too much. Whatever, I find it really hard to relate to boys and almost impossible to find a steady. Maybe I'm looking for what Mom and Dad had, this neat relationship that made them a special couple. And they're still in love and show affection after all these years. You'd think responsibilities and raising kinds like me and my lame brother would've changed them.

Boys. Who knows. I thought for a while Jimmy Alverez and I might be something. He was pretty nice. But he wouldn't stop calling me "Dude."

LANA

Parents divorcing often has a devastating impact on their children. Here Lana expresses this to her father.

LANA

I think a lotta times, when parents divorce, they don't have any idea how hard it is on their kids. I know when you and Mom split up I was crushed. Alluva sudden my whole world was turned upside down and overnight I went from feeling secure to being totally mixed up and afraid. I just couldn't believe what was happening. Alluva sudden I was all loose ends and confused and pissed and sad all at the same time. And it affected my schoolwork and everything. I went from a good student to sub-defective.

I should've seen it coming. I mean, you guys were arguing a lot and stuff and some nights I could hear you screaming at each other in your bedroom. And then for days you'd go without speaking. I tried to get between you and make things better, but nothing I did seemed to make any difference. I should've been able to keep you together. Sometimes I think maybe it was my fault. Maybe it was something I did that made you mad

5

at each other. (*Pause*.) I know, I know, but I think about it a lot. Blame myself, you know.

Now Mom and I are living in a condo because when you guys got divorced, you had to sell the house and split things up.

Do you realize the only time I see you now is on weekends, when you come by and blow the horn? Hey, you won't even come to the door.

Once we were a family, Dad. Now we're nothing.

BILLIE

She feels neglected by her father and in this speech expresses
her need for his attention and understanding.

BILLIE

Look, Dad, I need for us to be closer, you know. Seems like you never have enough time for me. (*Beat.*) Yeah, I know you're real busy and all, I know that. I know you have to work a lot to support us and everything, but still, I think you oughtta make some time for your daughter. I am here, you know, I exist. Although sometimes I don't feel like it. Seems like all you have time for is Jerry and hockey. You're not a father anymore, you're, like, a Hockey Dad. (*Beat.*) Yeah, I know, but I can't help it if I'm not athletic. Maybe I should've been born a boy. (*Beat.*) Okay, all right, but this is how I feel. Like I don't count, you know, like I come in second best, like I'm not part you. What about *me?* What about *my* interests. What about *my* feelings?

Lemme ask you: Why does my older brother get all the attention? (*Beat.*) Oh, really? Have you ever taken time to think about it? I have interests, too, you know. Like my ballet and

7

music and stuff. But do I get any support from anyone else around here but Mom? No. You didn't even take time to come to my last recital. (*Beat.*) I know you were out of town. But you know what? You could have postponed it for another day. If you really wanted to be there you'd've found a way, you'd've found a way. You sure don't miss any of Jerry's hockey games.

All I'm saying, Dad, is that I want a little attention. I need it. It's important to me. I need you to take an interest in me. I need to know you love me. I need to feel special.

SALLY

Sally realizes that one way to a boy's heart is through intelligence.

SALLY

I'm smart? Hey, thanks. But not always. In fact, at one time I wasn't into school at all. Didn't care. (*Pause.*) No, really, I was all about hanging with my friends and styles and cute guys. When it came to studies I was pretty loopy. I never studied and I just got by. I don't know how I ever got to high school. Then I met Greg.

Greg is super handsome and dresses cool and is captain of the football team. He's also a straight-A student—the last thing you'd think about a person like that. We met when he helped me get my money back out of a defective Pepsi machine. He couldn't have been more helpful. But the thing that impressed me most about him was that he was such a gentleman, not like a lot of guys who are good-looking and full of themselves and obnoxious. He wasn't any of this.

When he helped me out he had to put down an arm-load of books. It was like he was carrying around a library, you know. Me? I wasn't carrying anything but an attitude. To me books were, like, fearsome.

We started talking about stuff and it turned out we had a lot in common. Everything except schoolwork, that is. He was taking philosophy and French and weird math. When he asked me what I was interested in, I was, like, duh. I was barely getting through gym. So I faked it and he walked me to the bus stop and asked me for a date. Wow. And this is when I realized, if I wanted to go beyond a date, that is, I'd better get serious in the studies department. I mean, I couldn't fake it forever. Right? And I didn't want to blow a relationship with the coolest guy in school.

So I started in studying and getting better grades. Now I don't feel like a stupid dork around Greg anymore. Now I'm his equal. Also his steady girlfriend.

LORAINE

Loraine unloads her feelings on an over-protective parent.

LORAINE

You know what, Mom? You're smothering me, you're all over me, okay? You gotta stop watching over me like I'm some kid, a baby. (*Beat.*) Oh, yeah? Well, you're suffocating me. Look, I realize you think you're doing the right thing, but it's like you don't trust me to make my own decisions. How you think this makes me feel? Face it, you're not letting me grow up, take responsibility. What is it with you, anyway? Maybe your mother was all over you too. Well . . . I'm not going to let you pass it along to me; your insecurities and fears and worries. You gotta back off.

You know what you are, Mother? You're a helicopter mom, hovering over my life and sucking the freedom out of me. Look, I can understand to a degree, with all the crazy stuff going down these days, but I can't live in a cocoon and run away from life. Hell, everything has risks. And a person can't run away from reality.

11

If you had any confidence in me, you'd know I'm not going to do anything crazy. Believe it or not, I'm more adult than you think I am. In fact, lately, I think I'm more adult than you. (*Beat.*) Oh really? You think protecting your daughter from your imaginary fears is adult behavior? You think reading my private mail it rational? I know as long as I live here I've got to respect certain rules, but I can't be expected to become a prisoner because of your far-out fears and suspicions. Hey, you've become totally paranoid.

So please, Mother, respect my judgment and my privacy. Stop being a helicopter mom.

LAURIE

A rebellious Mary doesn't realize the importance of family and the need for discipline in her life. Here Laurie sets her straight.

LAURIE

That's really stupid, Mary. What a lame thing to say. Do you realize how important your family is, how much you need their support right now? (*Beat.*) Hey, I'm no angel, I never said that. But I still realize that there are rules, you know. Girls our age can't go totally against our parents. (*Beat.*) Oh, yeah? Bull. You're going out of your way to be obnoxious, to be different, to be off-the-wall. You're working at it.

I don't blame your mom for setting limits. (*Beat.*) She's *not* being a jailer. Can't you see this? She just knows that at this time of your life you need some kind of discipline. She's not being a jailer, she loves you. So you have to be home by eleven. So big deal. So you're expected to keep your room neat. So you're not allowed to date some guy who's twenty-three years old. You think this is unreasonable? Get real.

I think it's time you grow up and accept the value of the word No. It's not like your mom and dad are being unreasonable. Hey, you've got way more freedom than me. If I came home at one in the morning, I'd get it good. And I should. No one our age should be hanging that late.

You're problem is you're all about Me. Me, me, me! And it's not attractive and it's not cool and it's not healthy—it's sick. It's time to trade in the Mes for some Thems. You keep blowing off your family and you're gonna wind up blowing away the best thing in your life.

TAMMY

It's 9:00 PM and Tammy is fed up with not being fed. Here she voices her frustration regarding her date's indecisiveness.

TAMMY

Look . . . Chinese is cool. Italian is cool. German is cool. Russian is cool. Mexican is awesome. Sushi is wonderful. At this point, I don't really care. Even a greasy hamburger would be beautiful. A double bacon-cheeseburger, blood-rare on a soggy bun—even this will do. Even though I don't eat meat, haven't put meat in my mouth for over a year, although I'm very strict in this department, and even though the very thought of meat gives me diarrhea, I don't care. I'm so hungry I'm ready to eat the knobs off your car radio.

We've been driving around for over two hours. It's almost nine o'clock. And I think it's about time you made up your mind where we're going to eat. We go in the Japanese place, you didn't like the look of the waitress—dirty fingernails. So, we get up and leave. Then we walk out of Roma Italiano because they seated us too close to the kitchen. Hey, right now I wish I were *in* the kitchen. Then we drive all the way to River-

15

dale to the Chez Montmartre. And here you really flip because the guy at the next table says there's fur in his rabbit. This is ridiculous. Besides, you didn't have to order rabbit. You could have ordered the *coq au vin* or the coquilles or the scallops. Or what about French fries? You can't go wrong with French fries in a French restaurant. And French fries are totally furless.

Then we drag all the way back to Roma Italiano where you get into a thing with the *maitre d'* because there's an hour wait. What'd you expect? If we'd stayed put the first time, we'd be full of pasta and belching our way to a movie instead of driving around in circles with our bellies kissing our spines.

(*Pointing.*) Hey! Stop! Stop the car! Pull over! There's a McDonald's.

STELLA

Stella thinks she has finally found a way to defeat her father's Victorian ideas.

STELLA

So I tell 'im, "Dad, this isn't the end of the world. The house will still be standing tomorrow." Be he's all, "I'm not standing for you getting a tattoo, it's degenerate." I try to tell him if that's the case, how come some of the biggest movie and rock stars are into tattoos? He's all, "Quit using the term 'into.'" He's so past tense it isn't funny. I never realized how retarded he is.

I went through the same thing when I wanted to have my ears pierced. He was totally against this too. Mom and I pleaded with him for six months. Finally we just went ahead and had it done. He didn't even notice for over a week.

If it wasn't for my mom, I'd look like a total throwback. She's really up on new styles and stuff—really progressive. And she actually likes tattoos. But Dad . . . a Neanderthal. I think it comes from him being stressed out about the stock market. He's all about dollar signs. But when it comes to teen-ager stuff he's living in the Middle Ages.

What am I gonna do, Sandy? Even Mom can't figure this one out. (*Beat.*) What? No way. Mom's not that liberal. (*Beat.*) You really think so? You think if she gets one too he couldn't say anything? Hey, know what? I gotta felling she'll go for it. Something nice and discrete on her butt, that is. Yeah. I'll ask her today. (*Beat.*) Hey . . . I wonder how she feels about belly-button rings?

FRANCES

A person can't force a relationship to happen.

FRANCES

So what's the big deal? (*Beat.*) I know, but a lotta girls don't have boyfriends. So lighten up and relax. Look, I didn't have a boyfriend till this year. (*Beat.*) Yeah, really. Jimmy and I didn't hook up till after Christmas, so I know what you're going through. I felt the same way. It seemed like everyone was making it with their love life but me. I was getting real morose and down on myself and I started worrying about my looks and personality and everything. I was a total mess.

I even talked it over with my Mum. (*Beat.*) Sure, of course I talk to her about stuff. Why not? Who else you going to turn to, some total stranger? She was really cool and understanding and told me how she went through the same thing when she was young and how it affected her self-esteem and all and had her totally twisted. She said she didn't have a steady boyfriend till college. (*Beat.*) I know it sounds bizarre, but the point is, in time she met the right guy who, believe it or not, turned out to be my father. Neat, huh?

19

So don't go getting mental over it. Don't freak. You'll meet some guy before you know it, when you least expect it. But you can't push it. (*Beat.*) Will you stop it? You're *not* gonna be left behind. Behind what? Get over it, okay? Ya know, Julie, come to think if it, maybe you're better off. Me being with Jimmy every minute of the day is becoming a big pain in the butt.

JANET

Janet is furious over her sister's invasion of her privacy.

JANET

(*Upon entering, surprised to find her sister in her room.*) Hey, what the hell you doing in here? You have no business in my room, you little creep! This is, in case you hadn't thought of it, my own private space, not a public restroom. Do I come into your room when you're away? Do I come in your room and snoop around through your stuff, you nosy little weasel? Besides, what business have you got in here, anyway? None! You're just a nosy little rat who gets off on prying. I've told Mom a thousand times to keep you outts here. I guess I'm going to have to keep the door locked. (*Beat.*) C'mon, don't give me that. Besides, what would your stupid CDs be doing in my room? You think I'd take them? Why would I wanna listen to any of that junk? Your taste sucks!

Look, you can get away with lying. You can get away with trashing the bathroom. You can get way with not doing your share of the housework. You can get away with murder. But you can't get away with coming into my room when I'm not here. This if off limits, understand? Or are you too bone-headed or just too plain stubborn to get it? Well, whatever, you'd better remember, because the next time I catch you in here, I'm coming to your room and turning it upside down.

Now . . . get out!

ELAINE

Elaine's date is far from a big spender.

ELAINE

First off, he doesn't have a car, so he rode all the way across town to pick me up. Then we have to ride the bus to the Cineplex. And from where I live we have to transfer. Then, guess what, he goofed up on the movie time so we get there before it starts. Which means we have to hang out in the lobby watching fat people get double butter on their popcorn. So we sit there with nothing to say for at least twenty minutes. He wasn't much for conversation. I tried to get him involved, but he was all "duh." Boring. It was like dating my uncle Harold, who has this serious hearing problem. He also didn't offer to buy any refreshments.

After the movie he suggests we go over to Millers' for ice cream. So we have to walk five blocks. When we get there, I order the Chocolate Monster and he asks for a glass of water. This is when I finally realize he's cheap. He left the waitress a quarter. (*Pause.*) No, I'm not kidding. It was totally embarrassing. When we got ready to leave, when he wasn't looking, I slipped her a dollar.

Then we have to walk another five blocks to the bus stop, where I stand freezing my butt off while he goes on about stamp collecting. I'll bet he steams them off envelopes because I can't imagine him paying for them. He said this time he was going to ask the bus driver if there was a student discount. And he did. When we get on the bus he gets into this big thing about the fare. Can you imagine?

When we get to my stop he doesn't get off with me. Thank God. We say goodbye on the bus and says he'll phone me. Which I don't think I have to worry about because it's a toll call.

FRANCINE

She is totally against her mother having cosmetic surgery.

FRANCINE

Lately my mom's all about aging. Is your mom all about aging too? (*Pause.*) She is? Wow. I guess maybe it's a mid-life thing. My mom's always looking in the mirror and messing with herself and poking at her eyes and pulling at her chin. If she didn't have wrinkles she'd get them from pulling at her face all the time. I don't get it, you know. I mean, she isn't that old. But she's got this thing about her looks and is talking about having a facelift. I think she's nuts and my dad says it's way too expensive. Besides, he says he likes her the way she is. So do I. I hate to see her screw herself up.

Most people I see with facelifts look totally gross. Like Janet Pierce's mom. (*Pause.*) Have you seen her? (*Pause.*) You haven't? Hey, she's had cosmetic surgery and now she looks like a horror movie, now she has this puppet face and skin like polished marble.

The problem is, most women overdo. They start out talking about a little nip and tuck and wind up getting this total over-

25

haul: new nose, chin job, eyelids raised, neck tightened—the works. And they end up looking like pounded beef steak.

And you can always tell a face job too. They're like toupees: Even though some are pretty good, you can still spot 'em a mile away. And the hands are a dead giveaway Here you have this person with a face like a Halloween mask with these weasely old hands. Of course, some older women wear little white gloves, which make 'em look like a facelifted Minnie Mouse.

I told Mom what I thought; that it was a waste of time and that it wouldn't stop her from getting older. Besides, eventually she'd bag out anyway and have to get more surgery, which would make her look even more bizarre. I told her to be like my grandma and don't mess with herself. My grandma is really wrinkled, but I think she's beautiful.

ESTHER

A teenager's road is not always smooth.

ESTHER

It's sometimes really hard being a teenager in love. Because things don't always go smooth, ya know. I mean, sometimes you're very loving and then sometimes you get into these totally ridiculous fights like because of jealously and stuff. And when you quarrel it almost breaks your heart because you're afraid you'll break up. It's, like, one day you're happy and everything is cool and you can't keep your hands off each other, and the next day you're sad and angry to the point you almost feel like dying. Seems like it's hard to keep things on an even keel.

I wonder if it's just teenagers who feel like this. Maybe this is the way it is with older people too. Maybe they have the same problems. Like my mom and dad. Most of the time they're loving, but every now and then they get into a pretty bad place with each other—mostly over money.

Last night, at the Battle of the Bands, Dan got real chummy with Darlene Harding, got overly friendly it seemed like to me.

During breaks he hung out with her acting all silly and stupid. The way he behaved really hurt me. And when I bitched to him, he was all apologies and laughing and evasive. During the band's last set I walked out. When I got home I went straight to my room and cried myself to sleep.

If we break up I know I'll be lonely and depressed. And even though we'd no longer be a couple, I know I'd go on loving him.

It's not easy being a teenager in love.

BRYNN

Brynn attempts to get across to her parents the necessity for openness regarding teenage sex.

BRYNN

. . . But you can't go around denying it like a couple of ostriches with your heads in the sand. Sex is out there. It's everywhere. What about movies and TV and music? Sure, a lottta kids can hold off but most don't want to anymore. The majority of teens wanna have sex, are interested in it. So it's something we gotta deal with instead of running away from it and saying stuff like, "It's just a matter of abstinence." Well, it isn't just a "matter of abstinence" and, anyway, preaching it isn't gonna stop people from having sex. And if you keep pushing just abstinence without including sex education, well, then kids aren't gonna be prepared. They're not gonna have any idea about the facts. It's a whole lot better to expose us to sex and inform us about the use of birth control and condoms, to let us know there are people out there we can call. You can't run away from the truth, and it's not right to have kids thinking these feelings they have aren't natural.

29

Personally I'd like to wait for someone who means something to me. I'd like it to be spiritual, ya know. And I'm afraid to take chances. And when you're a girl you have to worry about a lot more than STDs, which are huge, you gotta worry about getting pregnant and getting stuck with a baby that'll change your whole life.

Another thing: I shouldn't have to rely on you guys for information, I should be more informed in sex-ed. And besides, you don't seem to understand how I feel about sex, how serious it is. If you did, you'd stop embarrassing me with off-the-wall stuff about how it was when you were young. Believe it or not, things have changed. Sex is out there. Kids today just don't sit around eating Gummy Bears.

BIANCA

She understands the seriousness of drinking and driving and her friend's erratic, alcoholic behavior. Here she takes her to task regarding her irresponsible ways.

BIANCA

Look, I'm not about to go getting wacked because you do. You wanna get loaded, it's your business, but when it comes to who's driving, it's gonna be me, all right? Hey, I really love you, okay? So don't get all bent outta shape about what I'm gonna say. It's an awkward subject, but I gotta bring it up.

You have any idea how much you've been drinking lately? You have any idea how wasted you get and how much you're embarrassing yourself? And your behavior's dangerous too. Because, when you drink, you get crazy and reckless and out of control. Like the other night at Mary's when you started throwing stuff. You may have thought it was cute, but it wasn't, it was totally unacceptable. Then you go and pass out. You think this is cool? Well, you need to know right now that it's *not* cool.

What is it with you? You got problems at home? Are you depressed or something? If so, you need to talk with someone. I'm worried about you, and I'm not the only one. So you gotta get help, and the sooner the better before you screw up totally and get yourself in a place where you won't be able to get out.

To be honest, I don't feel safe around you anymore, I don't feel comfortable because I never know what you're going to do. And there's no way I'm gonna let you drive. Hell, you can barely stand up.

I don't mean to rag on you, but you're not the person I made friends with when I met you. You were straight then. Now look at you, you're a drunken mess. So forget about getting behind the wheel.

Gimme the damn keys!

CHRIS

Chris and her mother's verbal battles have taken an emotional toll and gotten to the point where they can no longer be tolerated.

CHRIS

Hell no! Hell no, it isn't normal. What's normal about verbal abuse? About a kid and her mother screaming at each other day after day? You think it's normal for me to call you a self-centered bitch? You think it's normal for you to call me a slut? You think it's a good thing that I hate you? (*Beat.*) Yeah, even though I love you I hate you at the same time.

Even though sometimes we get along okay, most of the time don't make it. Mothers and daughters should get along good all the time. (*Beat.*) How else do you think I'd feel? You humiliate me, tell me I'm a loser and a failure, embarrass me in front of my friends, run me down every chance you get. It's no wonder I'm always in a negative place. It's no wonder my friends won't come to the house anymore. Who in their right mind wants be in the middle of a family fight?

I can understand why Dad left. You did the very same thing to him. Ragged on him constantly, always finding fault, never happy unless you were beating up on him about money and stuff. Nothing was ever good enough, you wanted more, a better house, better jewelry. It's no wonder he worked late and found stuff to do on the weekends. He needed to get away from you being on his case night and day. He's lucky, he got the hell out. And I have to figure out a way to get out too, get out before something really bad happens.

JANET

Janet suspects that Jerry's need to control and humiliate her is because she will not relent to sex.

JANET

You haven't changed, Jerry. Haven't changed, not really. I should've listened to my parents when they told me not to see you anymore. But I didn't, and I took you back because you promised me things would be different this time. But nothing's changed, it's the same old same old. You're still calling me names and telling me I'm not worth anything and telling me not to see my friends. And I can't even look at anyone else without you coming off the wall. Sometimes I wonder why you wanna go with me if I'm so defective. I guess maybe it's because I'm the only one who'll put up with your abuse. Hey. Forget it!

You may think I'm gonna hang with this, but I'm not into it anymore, Jerry, I can't take being put down and humiliated and controlled. (*Beat.*) Yeah, yeah. That sounds good but I don't believe it.

I think at the bottom of it is that I won't do it with you. I think this is the reason you need to yell at me and criticize me all the time. I think it's because I won't let you, as you say, "Hit a home run." Well . . . I'm not ready for "a home run" right now. I'm not comfortable with it. I know a lot of girls are, but it's my body and I'm not ready for it. If this is what's behind your putting me down all the time, my advice for you is to go find some biker chick.

EVELYN

Evelyn employs irony as a means of making her point with her profligate mother.

EVELYN

Yeah, like sure, Mother. It's gonna be totally neat being broke. Wonderful. Super. Poverty's delightful. Nothing like living on the edge without gas and electricity. It'll be neat being primitive. We can forage for food and make our own clothing. Hey, I can't wait. And I'm sure *you'll* love it, too. *S-u-u-u-r-e* you will.

It'll be an exciting new lifestyle for you. No more Gucci. No more shows. No more trips to Europe. No more daily martini klatches at The Plaza. No more summers at the beach. But who needs all that, right? Not you, n-o-o-o-o-o. Oh no—you're independent now. This is the life. Being broke is where it's at.

I think it was just brilliant not to save a dime and to spend like crazy. I mean, after all, what's money for, anyway? Like the ten thousand you blew on the Halloween party. Cute. You could have been a little sensible, invested, planned a little. But, what the hell, we were "in," we were "slammin."

This is gonna to be the *real* life. It'll be great not having a car. Walking's one of the healthiest things a person can do. Next summer we can walk up to the beach and check out the garbage along the way. And you can walk to the welfare office. And I'm sure you're going to love working. I hear there's a real glamour position open at Wal-Mart making keys.

Yes, Mommy dear, this is gonna to be a wonderful, beautiful adventure. Hey, we can look on it as a test to see if we can make it below the poverty level. Just think of the advantages. Now we'll be able to get next to street people and the homeless and hobnob with the lower crust. Just think of it, big spender. Hey! Isn't the thought of being poor exciting?

ADRIENNE

Adrienne expresses her inner thoughts of loneliness through her diary.

ADRIENNE

(She finishes writing in her diary, drops her pen, sits back, and reads aloud what she has written.)

Dear Diary,

I think it's about time I got stuff off my chest. And because I don't have a close friend to talk to, I'll talk to you.

My life here sucks. I don't have friends because I moved here from California about six months ago; moved from where it's nice and sunny and warm to where it's cold and rainy and the sun almost never shines. I really miss my old school and my teachers and my old neighborhood. And I miss being really tight with someone. I have a couple of acquaintances I met at school, but it's not like I'm very close to them. They're okay, I guess, but I don't feel close enough to them to tell them how I really feel about things. Before I had a special, super friend who I could talk to about anything. We didn't have any secrets.

I've tried to talk to my parents about how unhappy I am, but they don't take me seriously. They just kinda shrug it off and tell me I'm making too much of everything and that I'll be okay in time. Well, after six months I still feel depressed. I still miss my life and my friends and my boyfriend, who I think about all the time. We keep in touch by telephone and email, but this doesn't make up for not seeing him. I wonder a lot about what he's doing and worry he'll meet someone else.

I think moving is a lot harder on kids than it is on adults. I know it's been hard on me. Mom and Dad seem to be happy, but I can't seem to adjust. Maybe things'll get better. I sure hope so, because every day it's like I'm dying inside. (*She closes the diary and lays it aside.*)

JUDY

It's impossible for Judy to meet her mother's expectations.

JUDY

You know what my problem is? You're perfect. (*Beat.*) But you are. You're tall and thin and beautiful and I can't compete. How you expect me to? But you do, and this is the problem. (*Beat.*) Oh, yes you do. You ever stop to realize how much pressure you put on me? I don't think you have any idea. It's not like you say mean stuff, or anything. It's the way you expect me to be all these things you are. Well, I can't be anything but me. How do you think it makes me feel that I can't measure up to you, that I can't be outgoing and forceful and happy all the time?

Why can't you just accept me for what I am? (*Beat.*) But you don't, Mom. I'm sure you love me and all that, but, at the same time, you're driving me totally crazy. Like pushing me to go out with Adam Cruz because you think he's cute. I can't stand Adam Cruz, he makes me sick. Ew! But you've got this thing about me not being popular. Look, just because you're in every club in the city doesn't mean I'm into being Ms. Person-

41

ality. Besides, I'm not comfortable with hanging out and being with a lot of people.

You'd think you'd be happy I'm not obsessing about boys. But you aren't. And you know why? Because when you were in high school you were Homecoming Queen and super-organizer and cheerleader and Little Ms. Everything. Well, sorry, but this isn't me and the sooner you realize it, the happier we'll both be.

Allow me to have a life. Puleeze!

JASMINE

Jasmine assuages her friend's negative feelings because of acne.

JASMINE

But you gotta lighten up, Jill, it isn't the end of the world. Hey, everybody has acne, all teenagers go through it. Acne sucks, so what else is new? Acne is totally foul. Besides, what's the big deal. Look at you otherwise. Great body, nice boobs. You think with those legs a guy's gonna be turned off because of your acne? What if you had pipe stems? These you have for life. Acne clears up, bad legs don't.

Remember how I looked last year? Like my face was this city of zits, okay? And I felt terrible and ugly and embarrassed. I wished I coulda switched heads with somebody. It was like I couldn't look in the mirror, because every time I did I would break down and cry. And I didn't wanna leave the house. I was like this prisoner to pimples, you know. I was like wanting to die. I was in a totally negative place.

I was thinking about maybe becoming a hermit until my mom forced me to go to a dermatologist. She was pretty cool.

So told me that half the kids my age have acne and that my skin problem was normal and would go away. She told me if I'd stop looking in the mirror and start looking around I'd discover a lot of my friends had the same problem, and that they probably felt just like I did. She also gave me a prescription for this cream and told me how to properly wash my face and stuff. Now I don't have a single zit.

I also don't have your boobs.

ABBY

Even though she has HIV, Abby is thankful for having a loving, understanding boyfriend.

ABBY

Why do I love him? (*Pause.*) I love Chris because, you know, he's just awesome. Because he's special and makes me feel special too. And he never ever puts pressure on me because I have HIV, never brings it up and this is very cool.

I have a lotta guilt about having HIV, you know, although I never had anything to with it because it was something I picked up when they gave me this infected blood after a car wreck. But still I carry around these feelings that I'm not as normal as other girls. And then there's the pressure of knowing I'm not totally healthy.

But Chris never lets it, you know, get in the way of our relationship because he loves me in spite of the HIV, he understands. And he's had a bunch of pressure from his mom and dad about going with me. He told them I was infected even though he didn't have to. He said he didn't want to be carrying around a secret and that he didn't care what they thought anyway. This is another reason I love him; he's not all self-centered and I'm more important to him than what people think of him going with me.

And Chris makes me feel beautiful too. He's all about complementing me, and even when he doesn't tell me he let's me know that he thinks I'm special by the way he acts toward me—very respectful and caring. I've never thought I had super looks, or an amazing bod, but Chris make me feel like I do.

When I'm with Chris I'm, you know, relaxed because he's all very casual and laid-back. When I'm stressed-out about something, he sometimes holds me close and calms me down. His warm body next to mine is like a soothing thing. How cool is this?

I'm lucky, I guess. Even though I have HIV I have someone I love who loves me too.

LYNN

Her parents have complained to her school about their explicit teaching with respect to teenage sex. Embarrassed by this and fed up with their yesterday's attitude toward the subject, Lynn attempts to wise them up in no uncertain terms.

LYNN

No, you're not. You're not being realistic. You're being close-minded and narrow and hiding your heads under a blanket. You two are totally amazing. (*Pause.*) Well, sorry, but this is the way it is and I think it's a good thing. And besides, do you think I don't know about sex? What they're doing in school is a good thing. You think you'd be for it instead of acting like a couple of dinosaurs. (*Pause.*) I'm sorry, but it's time you woke up about teenage sex. You can't go on fighting the truth. Over half the high school kids in the country have had sex. So far, I haven't, okay? This should make you feel some better. But you think I don't have urges and feelings? So far I've been holding off, but I can't give you a guarantee that I'm going to be celibate till I get married. Chances are this isn't going to happen. (*Beat.*)

47

That's lame thinking. There's a lot more to it than just saying "no." Why do you think we have sex education and a day-
care center? Why do you think we're told about safe sex and
condoms? Because kids make it together, that's why, have ba-
bies and have to drop out of school and screw up their lives.
And then there's STDs around like crazy which never gets
talked about out in the open. There's syphilis and all kinds of
diseases all over the place.

You go complaining to the school, sit around preaching abstinence like a couple of Pilgrims. Not giving kids all the
information there is is not only dumb, it's irresponsible. Hey!
Thank God the school's making us aware. Somebody has to.
Most parents don't. You two sure don't. Instead of complaining to the school, you should be complimenting them.

Lemme ask you something, okay? Did you two have sex before *you* were married?

PAM

Pam, the daughter of a meth-using mother, appeals to her estranged father for help.

PAM

Like, are you okay with this, with me bothering you at work? I mean, I didn't wanna . . . (*Pause.*) Oh, good. Cool. I didn't wanna mess up your day, or anything, you know, but I just had to talk to you about Mom. I know you guys are busted up, but I didn't know who else to talk to. (*Pause.*)

Yeah, well . . . um, it's like Mom's doing meth. (*Pause.*) No, I'm not kidding, she's been into it for some time now. I woulda come to you sooner, but I thought I could handle it, you know, I thought I owed it to her to hang in, but the whole scene's wearing me out. I come home from school and she's all hazed and agitated and loud and abusive. I can't bring my friends home anymore because it's too embarrassing.

I went to a few Nar-Anon meetings where I hooked up with other kids who have the same problem. And it's helped a lot, but the situation at home has gotten worse and Mom's gotten more demanding and louder and more critical to the point I can't stand to be in the same room with her anymore.

And the whole thing is really messing up my schoolwork too. It's to the point I can't get any homework done at home. I've been going to the library and over to Margo's after school so I can concentrate.

I thought maybe there's something you can do. Maybe you can go talk to her. (*Pause.*) Hey! Like I know you don't get along, but how about me? I need your help right now, I need you to step up. This whole thing is really, you know, messing up my life, messing with my mind.

I'm asking for your help, Dad. I know you may not like Mom anymore, okay? But what about your love for me?

RAE ANN

Rae Ann's friend, Rita, is very demanding of her boyfriend. Here she tells Rita she needs to back off of her lavish expectations and appreciate the comfort of his companionship.

RAE ANN

Ya know what I think? I think you're expecting too much. (*Pause.*) Yeah, expecting too much. *Way* too much. No guy has that kinda money, not unless he's Spencer Washburn, and who'd wanna date a dweeb like him? Imagine kissing Spencer Washburn? Ew!

You've got to chill, girl, before you go blowing your thing with Davey, before you turn him off with all your demands and stuff. And he's a cool dude, too. Everybody I know thinks he's really cute. And he really likes you, too. You're lucky. You could be dating some twisted freak, some jerk who gets off on slapping you around. Here you got a gentleman, someone who treats you nice and respects you and you're all bent out of shape because he doesn't have a bunch of money. So, big deal. (*Pause.*)

Hector doesn't have any money, but I could care less. The thing is, we get along good and agree on most stuff and we don't get into stupid arguments over nothing. Hey! He can't even afford a car, so we have to bus it. So what? (*Beat.*)

What? C'mon, that's crazy. You can't expect him to afford that. Tickets to that show are, like, fifty bucks a seat. Besides, who wants to sit through a bunch of fools jumping around dressed up like cats? You know what, Rita? Your priorities are totally foul.

Hector and I like to rent DVDs and get junk food and sit around on his couch—we don't need to be doing something all the time. Going places constantly and spending a bunch of money isn't all that important when you love somebody. The main thing is just being together.

MAVIS

Mavis has stopped obsessing over her small breasts and has accepted the uniqueness of her own body.

MAVIS

It used to be a major thing. I was always stressed about my boobs. I felt like I'd been short-changed, you know. I didn't feel normal. (*Pause.*) Yeah, yeah, sure, but you don't really have any idea. If I had boobs like you, I'd have a party. But I don't, okay? So it took me a long time to get over being little on top. I was always thinking about my boobs and wondering if they'd get any bigger the older I got. I was totally obsessing.

My Mom kept telling me that it was natural, that I would develop later on. But it never happened. It was panic time. This is the reason I usta flake outta gym all the time. I was too embarrassed to take off my clothes, get in the shower. I used to be a total mess about being exposed. I was hiding my boobs like they were criminals.

I tried everything and read everything I could get my hands on. For a while I tried these chest exercises but all I ever got was sore. Then I sent away for these mechanical things, but when I used them it grossed me out. And I bought lotions and creams of all kinds of junk, which turned out to be totally useless. Padded bras are pretty cool. At least they make me look like I have *something*, even though they're just pushing up a couple of pimples.

You can't believe how awful I felt. It was totally terrible. Until my Aunt Ruth had to have a double mastectomy. This really woke me up. Alluva sudden I realized, you know, that having small boobs wasn't all that important and that I had to start accepting my body for what it was. So I'm small, so what? At least I have breasts.

MARIA

Having recently lost her mother, Maria expresses her sense of loss, her fears and frustrations, to her guidance counselor.

MARIA

Like, you know, sometimes I don't know what I feel. Like sometimes I'm just kinda numb.

Why did she have to die, Ms. Stickney? Why did she have to go and die? It isn't fair. I mean, to die so young and leave me and my dad all alone. Sometimes, when I think about it, I get so damned mad I don't know what I'll do. It's like I wanna explode. Then, other times, I'm so sad and I cry and I feel so disorganized and alone that I . . . (*Holding back tears.*)

(*Recovering.*) She was told she had cancer over a year ago, that she only had a few months to live. But we couldn't believe it, we just couldn't face the fact she was going to die. She went through all kinds of treatments and was very brave up till . . . up till the end.

She spent the last week of her life in the hospital. She called me into her room about fifteen minutes before she died and we hugged and kissed and she told me to be brave and that she loved me. It was the hardest thing I've ever faced in my life. My dad and I were with her at the end.

Coming back to school has been really hard for me, having to go on with my life, but I know that keeping busy, keeping in touch with my friends, and staying involved is the best thing. Thank God, Ms. Stickney, I get to talk to you.

The hardest thing right now is trying to help my dad recover. He's taking it even harder than I am and sometimes I feel guilty that I'm not as sad as he is. Dad just can't seem to express his grief, you know, to get out all the sadness inside him. Sometimes I feel like saying to him "Snap out of it," but I don't say anything outta respect for his feelings.

I'm sure things'll get better in time, but right now I feel empty and afraid. It's hard to face the fact that I'll never see my Mom again.

HILARY

Even though Hilary enjoys hanging with her friends, her first priority is family.

HILARY

I know you and Ramona get pissed because I wanna hang with my family a lot. But, know what? I'm all about family because I know this is the most important thing I got going. Like, hey, yeah, I got a little brother who's a pain in the butt and an older sister who thinks she's a rock star, but still, most of the time, they're pretty cool. And even though my parents are strict and I think a lot of their rules really suck, I'm still okay with them because what they tell me makes sense, you know. (*Pause.*) Yeah, well, maybe . . . but I'd rather be tight with my family than like some kids who may as well be orphans. Like Marsha Dixon, who complains and bitches about her family all the time. You ever been to her house? Wow. They get off on screaming at each other and slamming doors and even throwing stuff, you know. No wonder Marsha's totally screwed up. (*Pause.*)

C'mon, it's not that I don't enjoy hanging with you guys, we have some slammin' times. It's just that I don't wanna put partying first, that's all.

It may sound loopy, but I really like the stuff I do with my family. Like taking walks together, sharing stories, playing together and stuff, going on picnics and taking summer vacations. Even doing simple things, little stuff together is cool.

Even though I don't like to do some of the things that I'm expected to, I feel like it's the right thing to do. Like I gotta go to my lame brother's school play this Saturday and sit around bored in a stuffy auditorium. And when it's over I'll tell him how good he was . . . even though he can't act.